19.93

P9-CFQ-490

Pebble™ Plus

Mighty Machines

Backhoes

by Linda D. Williams

Consulting Editor: Gail Saunders-Smith, PhD

Consultant: Debra Hilmerson, Member
American Society of Safety Engineers
Des Plaines, Illinois

Capstone
press

Mankato, Minnesota

Pebble Plus is published by Capstone Press
151 Good Counsel Drive, P.O. Box 669, Mankato, Minnesota 56002
www.capstonepress.com

1 2 3 4 5 6 09 08 07 06 05 04

Library of Congress Cataloging-in-Publication Data
Williams, Linda D.
   Backhoes / by Linda D. Williams.
   p. cm.—(Pebble plus: mighty machines)
   Includes bibliographical references and index.
   ISBN 0-7368-2592-4 (hardcover)
   1. Backhoes—Juvenile literature. [1. Backhoes.] I. Title. II. Series.
TA735.W55 2005
629.225—dc22   2003025762

Summary: Simple text and photographs present backhoes and the work they do.

Editorial Credits
Martha E. H. Rustad, editor; Molly Nei, series designer; Scott Thoms, photo researcher; Karen Hieb,
   product planning editor

Photo Credits
Capstone Press, 1
constructionphotography.com, 18–19
Corbis/Lester Lefkowitz, cover, 10–11
David R. Frazier Photolibrary, 6–7, 8–9, 12–13, 15
Folio Inc./Catherine Ursillo, 16–17; Mark Gibson, 20–21
Index Stock Imagery/Omni Photo Communications Inc., 4–5

Transportation
JE

Note to Parents and Teachers

The Mighty Machines series supports national standards related to science, technology,
and society. This book describes and illustrates backhoes. The images support early
readers in understanding the text. The repetition of words and phrases helps early
readers learn new words. This book also introduces early readers to subject-specific
vocabulary words, which are defined in the Glossary section. Early readers may need
assistance to read some words and to use the Table of Contents, Glossary, Read More,
Internet Sites, and Index/Word List sections of the book.

Word Count: 118
Early-Intervention Level: 11

Table of Contents

Backhoes

Backhoes dig and lift. Backhoes help make new roads and sidewalks.

Track backhoes move on rolling tracks. They dig holes with large buckets.

bucket

Backhoe loaders move on
tires. They dig with buckets.
They lift with loaders.

loader →

NORTH HAVEN MEMORIAL LIBRARY
NORTH HAVEN CT 06473

9

Parts of Backhoes

Backhoe buckets have
metal teeth. The teeth help
backhoe buckets dig.

teeth

Backhoe drivers sit in cabs.
Side legs help backhoes
stay steady.

cab

side leg

410D HEAVY LIFT

JOHN DEERE

13

Backhoe booms move like
an arm. Backhoe booms
move buckets in and out,
up and down.

boom

What Backhoes Do

Backhoes dig down deep
into the ground. They
scoop dirt and then swing
it high into the air.

17

Backhoes dump rocks
and dirt into trucks.
Backhoes fill train cars
with gravel and coal.

19

Mighty Machines

Backhoes dig and lift dirt
and rocks. Backhoes are
mighty machines.

Glossary

backhoe loader—a machine with a bucket for digging and a loader for lifting; a backhoe loader moves on tires.

boom—a metal arm that moves a backhoe bucket

bucket—a scoop on a backhoe; a bucket is on the end of a boom.

cab—an area for a driver to sit in a large truck or machine, such as a backhoe

side legs—a pair of metal bars on the sides of a backhoe; side legs keep backhoes from tipping over.

track—a wide metal or rubber belt that runs around wheels; track backhoes move on two tracks; tracks help backhoes move over rough ground.

track backhoe—a machine with a bucket for digging; a track backhoe moves on metal or rubber tracks.

Read More

Deschamps, Nicola. *Digger.* Machines at Work. New York: DK Publishing, 2004.

Jones, Melanie Davis. *Big Machines.* A Rookie Reader. New York: Children's Press, 2003.

Randolph, Joanne. *Backhoes.* Earth Movers. New York: PowerKids Press, 2002.

Internet Sites

FactHound offers a safe, fun way to find Internet sites related to this book. All of the sites on FactHound have been researched by our staff.

Here's how:

1. Visit *www.facthound.com*

2. Type in this special code **0736825924** for age-appropriate sites. Or enter a search word related to this book for a more general search.

3. Click on the **Fetch It** button.

FactHound will fetch the best sites for you!

Index/Word List